Give Yourself Permission to
GLOW

Felecia Alexander

Copyright © 2023 By Felecia Alexander

The content contained within this book may not be reproduced, duplicated, or transmitted in any form or retrieval system now known or to be invented without direct written permission from the author or publisher. Under no circumstances will any blame or legal responsibility be held against the publisher, or author, for any damages, reparation, or monetary loss due to the information contained within this book. Either directly or indirectly.

Legal Notice:

This book is copyright protected. This book is only for personal use. You cannot amend, distribute, sell, use, quote, or paraphrase any part of the content within this book without the author or publisher's consent. "Fair Use" means a summary or quote with appropriate credit to the author is permitted.

Disclaimer Notice:

Please note the information contained within this book is for educational purposes only. All effort has been executed to present accurate, up-to-date, reliable, and complete information. No warranties of any kind are declared or implied. Readers acknowledge that the author is not rendering legal, financial, medical, or professional advice. The content within this book has been derived from various sources. Please consult a qualified professional before attempting any techniques outlined in this book. By reading and using this book, the reader agrees that under no circumstances is the author responsible for any direct or indirect losses incurred due to the use of the information within this book, including, but not limited to, — errors, omissions, or inaccuracies.

EBOOK ISBN: 978-969-3292-93-0

PAPERBACK ISBN: 978-969-3292-94-7

HARDBACK ISBN: 978-969-3292-95-4

Dedication

I hope you enjoy this read. Writing this book brought so much joy and laughter as I can hear my granny's voice. Give yourself permission to glow is dedicated in honor of Maggie Johnson Alexander (1923 – 2017)

In memory of

TABLE OF CONTENTS

INTRODUCTION 1

GLOW 1 START FRESH 6

    Other Favorite Cleanser Products 8

    Time to Shed 8

    Other Favorite Products for Exfoliation 11

    Time to Restore 12

    Other Favorite Products for Moisturizing 15

GLOW 2 Healthy Deposit 17

    Eat Beauty-fully 17

    Let's Talk Veggies! 19

    Let's Add Some Color to the Palate! 21

    Drink Plenti-fully 22

GLOW 3 Beauty Sleep 27

    Time to Rest 27

    Beauty Sleep Tips 28

GLOW 4 Natural Replenishment 31

    Give the Sun Permission to Kiss Your Face 31

The Sun Can Be Seen As a Curse and a Gift. 32

GLOW 5 Self-Care 37

    Self-Love 37

    Treat Yourself 43

    Seek Help 45

    How Often Should You Visit a Board-Certificated Dermatologist? 45

    Why is Dermatology Important? 45

    Give Yourself Permission to Glow 46

Works Cited 49

Acknowledgement 53

THE AUTHOR 55

INTRODUCTION

Wow, you have great skin! You are glowing! What do you use on your face? What's your skincare routine? These are a few statements and questions I get asked frequently.

Greetings, my name is Felecia Alexander, raised in a quaint town on a plantation outside of Tallahassee, Fl, in Jefferson County, known as Monticello, population of 2,569. Monticello is named after the estate of the county's namesake, Thomas Jefferson. Yes, the President, Thomas Jefferson, hence the county courthouse was modeled, Jefferson County Courthouse.

You will hear me reference my grandparents a lot as they basically raised my sister and I while my mother completed her higher education.

My grandparents were sharecroppers for Dixie Plantation. Being raised on a plantation we relied on farming, natural resources, and spending wisely, so we didn't have a lot of money for expensive beauty products. It's instilled in me the need for utilizing natural resources, healthy eating, and having an active lifestyle as a great way to maintain youth. My grandparents lived long healthy lives—grandfather 104, and grandmother 93.

By no means am I a specialist of skincare; these tips are what work best for my skin type which is normal to dry. I must say I continued many of these home remedies just because my granny said so. It wasn't until I was older that I researched the benefits and effects of these tips.

Small town girl meets big city, Miami, FL in 1994 to attend Fashion School. Talk about culture shock! I waited a few years after high school before taking off to the big city until I figured out what I want to be when I grow up. I always had a flair for fashion, thanks to my mom, Mrs. Farrow my Home Economics teacher, and the 4-H Club for showing me how to sew. Since I had no natural flair for drawing, I attended International Fine Arts College, known today as Miami International University of Art & Design where I gained an Associates of Arts degree in Fashion Merchandising. Here I had my first experience with fashion trends and brand-name cosmetics, as I was involved in the production of fashion shows creating eye-catching visual displays to showcase the products. I continued on to St. Thomas University where I obtained a Bachelors in Communications.

As a child, every day held the promise of a new adventure. From imaginary quests in backyard bushes to bicycle expeditions. To this day, the adventure lives on. In 2010, I served as an overseas contractor supporting the US military then returned in 2019. My first deployment was to Afghanistan, living in a small container that accommodated two persons at a time—talk about minimalist living. This is where less is definitely required, but learning to take care of my face in those conditions was a must.

During a pause from contracting, I became an International Flight Attendant. As a result of flying trans-atlantic routes from the US to different countries, it's safe to say I'm still utilizing a moderate budget and buying fewer products.

Recently, I got an opportunity to go back overseas and support the US military in a different capacity. Of course it's vital that I continue to care for my face. I will be sharing with you my granny's tips and some of my favorite products.

I would advise doing a small patch test on your skin to ensure you do not have an adverse reaction. I hope these tips that I am going to share will enlighten your path of living a long bountiful, healthy, life with a GLOWING FACE.

GLOW 1

START FRESH

Let's Begin with a Clean Slate!

Cleanse and clean mean the same thing. To purify or remove dirt or impurities.

Apple cider vinegar (ACV) was used to cleanse and marinate meat back in those days, so what better way to cleanse your skin than to use it! If it was good for the meat, then it must be great as a skin cleanser. I remember playing outside while my grandmother would draw a bath in a huge tub on the porch to wash-up before coming inside for dinner. In my head, it was my swimming pool. My granny would also add a few drops of apple cider vinegar. I didn't know why, but I continued to cleanse my face with diluted

ACV and cool water. I place a few drops in the sink and use a face cloth to gently wash my face. Make sure you are using a clean face cloth.

Benefits

Apple cider vinegar is like a superfood; the list of benefits is limitless for your overall health. What makes it special for your face? *Acetic Acid* is the fermentation process that creates a compound in the vinegar which is well known for its antibacterial and antifungal properties. Here are a few benefits of using it:

- ❖ Removes oil, dirt, and other gunk
- ❖ Works as a toner as it serves as an astringent
- ❖ Spot treatment for blemishes
- ❖ Eliminates premature wrinkles as it tightens and strengthens the cells in the skin

- ❖ Has antimicrobial properties that have various organic acids. These acids have been effective in inhibiting bacterial growth
- ❖ Reduces acne as it balances the skin pH.

Other Favorite Cleanser Products

My on the go is CeraVe Hydrating Cream-to-Foam Cleanser for Normal to Dry Skin which I use with a silicone facial brush. It also comes in travel size and biodegradable cloth version great for removing make-up. It is accepted by the National Eczema Association.

Bonus: When traveling abroad and you find yourself in a situation where water is harsh or chemically treated, use bottled water as a last resort to rinsing your face.

Time to Shed

Exfoliate, to shed or remove dead skin or cells from the outer layer of your skin.

Back to my granny, if I was really dirty, she would apply a mix of baking soda to my elbows, knees, and feet; in an instant they would all be baby soft! Keep in mind you are removing dead skin cells, so be gentle. Treat your face like a baby, after all you want your skin to feel soft.

As an adult, I have become more invested in my skin. I started mixing baking soda and water into a paste and applying it as an exfoliator, once a week. Keep a fresh box of baking soda in your bathroom. I store mine in a mason jar, which you can get from the dollar store. Apply a little on your fingers, and gently rub in a circle motion. Be mindful of the eye area and rinsing with cold water. Voila! Just like that; baby soft!

Benefits
Baking Soda is a natural antiseptic with antibacterial properties and can serve as a superfood for your skin. It can be used as a paste for

shoulders/back acne, eczema, psoriasis, chickenpox, and ichthyosis, hair removal to name a few. Some of its benefits include:

- Removing dead skin cells
- Boosting your cleanser
- Softening your skin
- Can be combined with other natural products such as honey, green tea, essential oils
- Tackles oily skin
- Tightens pores
- Serves as spot treatment for acne (check with your dermatologist)
- Adds glow

However, there are some side effects worth mentioning. Due to the high level of alkaline chemical compound, baking soda can alter the natural pH of the skin, resulting in dryness of the skin, early onset of wrinkles, worsening acne breakouts, and skin irritation. Do a small patch test, as it might not be safe for everyone. And, of course, always, consult with your dermatologist.

Other Favorite Products for Exfoliation

My esthetician introduced me to Dermalogica Daily Microfoliant. It's a rice-based enzyme powder micro-exfoliator with very fine granules that make it great to mix with your facial cleanser as well. It is a bit pricey, but worth it, as a little goes a long way. It also comes in travel size.

I absolutely love this brand of natural products, Ancient Cosmetics. The "even skin healthy glow face scrub" is literally sunshine in a jar. It's a sugar scrub with ingredients such as very fine sugar, turmeric root powder, lemon, frankincense, argan, and safflower oil, and leucidal liquid radish root ferment. It is moderately priced, and a little goes along way. Like always, if you have sensitive skin, acne prone skin, or any skin condition, please check with your dermatologist before using it.

Time to Restore

Moisturize, to nourish, restore or add moisture to your skin.

Now that you've cleansed and exfoliated, it's time to restore. Did you know that skin is the largest organ of the body? So moisturizing is a crucial component of a youthful and glowing face. It is imperative that you do this daily, and ensure you stay hydrated. Make sure you're drinking plenty of water which we will explore in our Glow 2 chapter.

At midday, your skin oil production peaks, thereby losing that protective layer of natural oils. The best time to moisturize your skin is at night, because there is less oil production. It's important to replenish the water loss with a moisturizer overnight as the skin goes into renewal mode.

Granny used Vaseline from the "rooty to the tooty" which means everywhere. I literally looked like I was ready to be put in a frying pan.

Vaseline is more of a skin barrier, meaning it keeps dirt out and prevents moisture loss. Sorry granny, but this one I only kept for removing make-up, especially lipstick stains, and waterproof eyeliners, then I dab a little underneath the eyelid to reduce puffiness; along with rubbing some on my elbows, knees, feet, and hands.

According to Medial News Today, the Environmental Working Group (EWG), (2018), Vaseline is one of the petroleum jellies that has a low risk of exposing users to carcinogens and other dangerous ingredients. It is reported that some unrefined petroleum jelly can contain some potentially dangerous contaminants, so stick with a brand that you can trust such as Vaseline. Of course, if you have sensitive skin, acne prone, or any skin condition, please check with your dermatologist before utilizing.

I now use NOW Solutions grapeseed oil at night after cleansing or exfoliating to a damp face, and during the day as an additional moisturizer when traveling to cold climates along with my sunscreen.

Grapeseed oil is light weight, and full of vitamin E which locks in moisture and hydrates the outer layer of the skin which is needed to achieve a glowing skin.

Benefits
- Anti-inflammatory, antimicrobial, antioxidant which is great for acne outbreaks, and can be used as a topical treatment
- Improves elasticity and softness of the skin
- Evens out skin tone with an ingredient called proanthocyanidin which is a powerful antioxidant
- Can be taken orally

❖ Protects the skin from skin damage

Speaking of protecting the skin from sun damage—yes, dark skin does need protection—it is important to choose a moisturizer that has SPF. My all-time favorite is "BLACK GIRL SUNSCREEN – SPF 30", which I layer in the winter months or cold climates with grapeseed oil.

Other Favorite Products for Moisturizing

Black Girl Sunscreen applies evenly and smoothly, and it doesn't leave a white residue; even if you sweat and it wears well under make-up. It is moderately price, and comes in SPF 30, Matted SPF 45, SPF 50, and the formula for kids.

There are no substitutes for these products; they go everywhere with me. For short trips, I use travel sizes of grapeseed oil and Black Girl Sunscreen. On longer trips, I make sure I insert a small piece of cotton ball or plastic wrap under the top to prevent spillage.

Fenty Instant Reset Brightening Overnight Recovery Gel-Cream With Niacinamide + Kalahari Melon Oil is noncomedogenic and earth-conscious, as it comes in refillable packaging. It is an amazing product, which I purchased the mini size when the brand initially came out to try. A little goes along away as well, and it leaves you with a dewy look.

Bonus: I use rosewater when traveling, especially in hot climates to help hydrate my skin. You can add any essential oil of your choice, but choose wisely as you are applying it to your face. Lightly spray your face and instantly feel refreshed with an extra glow.

GLOW 2

Healthy Deposit

Eat Beauty-fully

A glowing face goes beyond the skin; it's much deeper. It is what you feed your body that's another important factor. Let's visit some of the foods I grew up on that will help you make a healthy deposit into glowing skin.

Growing up in the country was definitely a great advantage to having home grown vegetables and fruits. There was no McDonald's or Burger King in sight; our fast food was the rolling sto (store) man that would drive by and we could buy whatever fruits or vegetables we didn't grow and some windwheel and coconut cookies for five cents.

Here's some of my favorite foods in making a healthy deposit that I credit to date which contribute to a glowing face: To start with, Monticello is famous for growing watermelon; we even have a big festival "Watermelon Festival", which is a huge event attended by people from other towns, cities, and states. I was a runner up for Ms. Watermelon Queen in 1987. Gotta love small towns.

Watermelon is not only mouthwatering; it is said to clear blemishes, as well as smooth and improve skin elasticity. Watermelon also protects from the sun which means it can aid in fighting cancer.

From the succulent juiciness of watermelon, let's venture into the world of smaller, yet equally delightful, berries. While playing outside, we would gather the wild blackberries and raspberries that grew there. My grandparents planted blackberries in a little patch in the backyard. Nowadays, I'm running to pick them up from the supermarket; best time to buy them is when they're in season. It's pretty safe to say that all berries, especially blackberries, raspberries, and strawberries are a huge investment in making a healthy deposit for a glowing face.

Berries are very high in vitamin C, which makes them a strong antioxidant. Serving as a strong antioxidant helps to keep the collagen in the skin very healthy. They also contain anthocyanins and quercetin which contain anticancer, anti-inflammatory, and antimicrobial properties. In summary, it helps with inflammation, keeps the skin toned, and helps with a radiant glowing face.

Let's Talk Veggies!

We know that green leafy vegetables are overall good for the body, and thankfully, we had an abundance of it growing up. We could look out the back door and see rows of collards, turnips, mustard greens, strings beans, okra, and cucumbers, just to name a few.

The Greens—collard, turnip, and mustard greens—are members of the Brassica; a plant of genus group. Brassica contains high levels of vitamin C, A, E, K, as well as folate, calcium, iron, potassium and phosphorus which play a major role in achieving the "GLOW". Did you know that okra is a companion plant of the Brassica family? Okra is enriched with vitamin A and C, and polyphenols which is an antioxidant.

The benefits of the greens. Let's revisit the alphabet again, vitamin C enhances collagen, keeping skin tight; vitamin A is known for its anti-inflammatory properties that can help improve acne. It also has retinoids; which reduces fine lines and wrinkles; vitamin E provides support for acne and sun damaged skin.

You can imagine we had the greens and okra prepared in many different ways; fried, stewed, soups, etc., all of which I enjoy to this day. I must say way better when my mom or sister prepares them. Something about being back in my home town eating these soul food as we call it, brings out the flavor or, more likely, it's the love I know that went into preparing them.

Let's Add Some Color to the Palate!

If there were greens, you know there were sweet potatoes. Super fresh and sweet; you could wash them off and eat them straight from the ground.

The benefits of sweet potatoes are that it is high in beta-carotene which are useful for fighting free radicals and skin agers. They are also rich in vitamin C and vitamin E; essential components of a glowing face.

The benefits of tomato, are also a good source of vitamin C and antioxidants. Now you're on your way to a bright, shining face. Let's glow!

Drink Plenti-fully

I don't know about you, but all this food talk is making me thirsty. Let's jump right into our next healthy deposit!

There's no better hydrating agent than **WATER!** There are so many accounts for the amount of water we should be drinking. Some accounts say four to six, four to eight, four to 12 cups; there is no one answer to this because it varies from person to person, depending on many different factors such as gender, general health, environment, amount of exercise, if you are pregnant/breast-feeding, etc. All these things play a role in how much water you need in a day.

According to the Mayo Clinic (2022), "water is our body's principal chemical component and makes up about 50% - 70% of your body weight." Your body depends on water to survive.

Did you know that our blood consists of 90% water? By drinking water, the cells throughout your body become hydrated through the bloodstream, thus hydrating your skin.

This process flushes out impurities and toxins at the cellular level, preventing acne and giving your face a radiant glow.

The U.S. National Academies of Sciences, Engineering, and Medicine (Mayo Clinic 2022) determined that "healthy adult living in a temperate climate daily fluid intake should consist of:

- ❖ 15.5 cups (3.7 liters) of fluids a day for men
- ❖ 11.5 cups (2.7 liters) of fluids a day for women

This would include fluids from water, other beverages and food."

Listen to your body; consider if you are feeling thirsty, check your urine color to see if it's colorless or light yellow; consider the factors above; and when in doubt check with your physician.

I work out at least five times a week and presently work 6 days/12hour shift in a desert environment as a contractor. My intake is 2-3 liters of water including 10-14oz Branch Chain Amino Acids (BCAA), green teas, and coconut water preferable Grace and Iberia brand. Liquid I.V hydration multiplier packs, plain raw ginger, and lemon added to my water.

Benefits
- ❖ Gives the skin a smooth tone
- ❖ Increases elasticity, and tightens the skin thereby slowing down the appearance of wrinkles and lines
- ❖ Speeds up healing of blemishes such as sunburns
- ❖ Reduces puffiness in your face. If you stay hydrated, your body doesn't need to protect you by retaining water

- Prevents acne by balancing water and oil content on your face
- Keeps the skin from becoming dry and itchy

Drinking water simply is an amazing health deposit when it comes to a glowing face, as it restores your body's pH.

I know what you're thinking, "I hate drinking water, water is boring". Well here are some of my favorite ways to brighten up your water, hot or cold, for a glowing face:

- Lemon/lime/oranges
- Cucumber
- Pineapple
- Mint
- Basil
- Ginger

Bonus, if you want something with a little fizz, I recommend grapefruit or lime Perrier sparkling water. Add a pack of crystal light or squeeze of Mio and you got yourself a nice spritzer.

GLOW 3

Beauty Sleep

Time to Rest

Beauty Sleep is adequate sleep you need in order to feel good and look healthy.

Beauty sleep is just like water; you need it to survive. While sleeping, the skin restores and rebuilds to a healthy glow. It uses those hours to heal itself from the day's damage.

Just how much sleep is enough to get your beauty sleep? According to Sleep Foundation (2023) "seven to nine quality hours of sleep per night is ideal for 'beauty sleep'." Consistent with the Mayo Clinic (2022), "adults need seven or more hours a night". However, age and other factors can affect how many hours of sleep is needed. They also state that "if our sleep is frequently interrupted, you're not getting quality sleep. The quality of sleep is just as important as the quantity."

Beauty Sleep Tips

- ❖ Go to bed with a cleansed and moisturized face as we talked about in Glow 1
- ❖ Be consistent with your sleep schedule
- ❖ Maintain a comfortable temperature before climbing into bed
- ❖ Watch what you eat and drink before bed time
- ❖ Side note - Sleep Foundation (2023), excess alcohol and wine may aid with sleep onset, but it is likely to disrupt the sleep cycle. They can have a negative impact on your body as the liver enzymes need time to metabolize. This is different from person to person.

- ❖ On the good note, drinking in moderation and at least four hours before bedtime is generally safe. This gives the body time to metabolize the alcohol. Bottom line, listen to your body. I am sticking to my glass of red wine for all it's good benefits 😊

- ❖ Carve out time for a relaxing bath with all the trimmings and don't for get to moisturize

- ❖ Chamomile tea is nice

- ❖ Eliminate the use of electronic devices before bedtime and minimize light and noise

- ❖ Dark rooms allow your brain to produce melatonin hormones

- ❖ Melatonin is the body's natural magic pill. It creates a feeling of calmness and decreases anxiety

- ❖ Here's a BIGGIE: end your day before bed. If there are some tasks you didn't complete, its ok to do them the next day. I always remind myself of this.

Benefits
- ❖ Allows the skin to heal and restore
- ❖ Less stress decreases breakout like acne, blackheads, and pimples
- ❖ Decreases puffiness and dark circles
- ❖ Side note: elevating your head just a bit works great for back sleepers
- ❖ Produces collagen which helps our skin looking younger and reduces the appearance of wrinkles
- ❖ Increases blood flow to the skin which evens your skin tone giving it that glow

There are so many more helpful tips, but these are the ones I deemed worthy and like to incorporate for myself.

GLOW 4

Natural Replenishment

Give the Sun Permission to Kiss Your Face

Sun-kissed is the moment the right amount of sun shines upon your face, leaving the person with a tanned or bronzed appearance, and resulting in a healthy glow.

I would describe it as a heavenly experience when God cradles my head, blows softly on my face, and uses his power to create a perfectly crafted natural glow in tones of gold and bronze. It leaves such an impact that one can see a glowing light upon my face, it leaves me with a huge smile, and it leaves me filled with positive energy.

The Sun Can Be Seen As a Curse and a Gift.

The Curse

Potentially anything in excess is not good for you. The sun is not to be excluded. Let's talk science so we can understand the curse. According to News in Health (2014) the sun travels to Earth as a mixture of both visible and invisible rays or waves. Short waves (UVB rays, ultraviolet B, 280-30m) can travel deeper into the skin causing harm like sunburn, and cutaneous malignant melanoma (CMM).

These rays over time can cause premature aging, become less elastic, thickened, leathery, wrinkled, and thinned like tissue.

The strongest times of these UVB rays are between 10am-4pm depending on your location. At these times you should protect yourself more. Generously apply sunscreen to the exposed area about 15min before going outside, wear protective clothing, and seek shade. You can even check the UV Index issued by the National Weather Service and EPA. Environmental Protection Agency (EPA) (2023) reports "most common form cancer in the United States is skin cancer, more than 3.5 million new cases are diagnosed annually."

Ask yourself if you are a lover of the sun and if you overindulge. If the answer is yes, take a little extra time to evaluate your face and your entire skin, and if you notice any spots, moles, or abnormal growth, please check with your dermatologist. Make this a part of your annual checkup even as a preventative measure. Remember early detection of melanoma can save your life.

The Gift

We learn science behind the sun and how it travels to Earth as a mixture of both visible and invisible rays or waves. So, just as we have short waves, there are long waves (UVA, ultraviolet A, 320-

400nm). They are like radio waves and are harmless, according to News in Health (2014).

Bonus, studies by Georgetown University Medical Center (2016) researchers have found the sun is an immune booster. The sunlight makes hydrogen peroxide in the T cells. "Hydrogen peroxide is a compound that white blood cells release when they sense an infection in order to kill bacteria and to "call" T cells and other immune cells to mount an immune response."

Benefits
- ❖ Sunlight helps keep our sleep pattern on track so that you stay awake during the day and sleep soundly at night
- ❖ It boosts your mood, making you less stressed
- ❖ UV has anti-inflammatory effects, and helps to reduce swelling and redness

- ❖ UV light can help the healing process of some skin conditions. Always check with your dermatologist for further information
- ❖ Produces more melanin which creates the bronzer/golden skin tones

I permanently reside in South Florida, so I love being outside in the sun, whether it's running, cycling, beaching, art exhibiting and everything else the city has to offer. But I practice safety. Presently, I work out of the country in a desert environment, so there is even more reason for me to protect my skin.

The bottom line is enjoying natural replenishment in moderation and utilizing any protection measure to ensure your safety. It is very important to remember your sunscreen, hydrate, wear light clothing, expose yourself moderately during strongest UV periods (10-4pm), and be careful if you are taking medications that may contraindicate sun exposure. When in doubt, seek medical assistance from a dermatologist.

GLOW 5

Self-Care

Self-Care is a channel of rivers such as self-love, treating yourself, and seeking help which all lead to one body of water— you. You must protect your well-being and happiness by maintaining your body, mind, spirit, and soul especially during stressful periods.

Self-Love

Self-love is an attitude of appreciation for oneself that develops from actions that support your psychological, physical, and spiritual growth. Self-love means having a high regard for your own well-being and happiness. Self-love means taking care of your own needs and not sacrificing your well-being to please others. Self-love means not settling for less than you deserve.

Self-love is individualized. It's a personal journey, and it's taking stock of your mental, emotional, physical, spiritual well-being and treating yourself. GIVING YOURSELF PERMISSION TO GLOW.

Mental awareness is very important. According to the National Institute of Mental Health, "it affects how you think, feel, act, make choices, and relate to others." It's important to seek help when you are feeling overwhelmed, discouraged, unsure of circumstances, or whatever is making you feel disconnected to life.

What does seeking help look like? Talking with a professional, spiritual guidance, meditation, journaling, disconnecting from social media, electronic devices, etc. Try breath work and creating mindfulness to help manage and reduce stress.

Create a safe place for yourself emotionally. When I wake up, I always practice gratitude. I speak things out I am grateful for, and even set positive intentions throughout the day. Create and/or listen to affirmations, frequency vibrations, or relaxing music. If you're a task person like me and suffer from the alphabet "OCD", set priorities, make a list and if you don't complete them, again know it's ok to roll them over into the next day because you get to start over (NOTE TO SELF). Do this and watch how your day will flourish, so when those not so pleasant moments happen, you will be better at coping with them.

Creating a safe place is also giving yourself permission to say "NO", and set boundaries that will not allow others to take advantage of your space. It's worth mentioning again, know when to "SEEK HELP."

Physical well-being includes all the things we discuss in taking care of your body:

- ❖ Start Fresh – cleanse, exfoliate, and moisturize
- ❖ Eat Beauty-fully – eat nourishing foods
- ❖ Drink Plentifully – stay hydrated
- ❖ Get enough Beauty Sleep

Include exercise as well, even if its small amounts. Start with a walk, try group activities to help you get started, or get a personal trainer. Just get moving.

Overall, exercise improves your mental health which reduces stress and depression, boosts your mood, and improves your self-esteem. It also improves blood flow which we know helps regenerate, repair, and slows premature signs of aging. All of these are factors that contribute to a glowing face.

Spiritual well-being empowers you in your journey through life. It gives you a sense of purpose, it helps you emotionally process stressors, and overall enhances your well-being. My spiritual well-being is expressing gratitude when I wake. I give thanks to God for EVERYTHING! I say a prayer, and have a daily devotional message/bible verse I receive every day that teaches me how to be more Christ-like. It's connecting with people on a higher level of positivity; it's seeking knowledge and wisdom, encouragement, giving, forgiving, apologizing, and having hope and faith, accepting the things that I cannot change. It's about being a better me.

Spiritual well-being has two components, "religious well-being, which refers to the connection with God or a higher being, and existential well-being, which pertains to the meaning and purpose in life."

❖ Religious well-being: whatever you believe in as your higher being, set aside time to connect and deepen your relationship with it. Let it be a guide to help you love yourself and others. Let it be an impact on how you treat yourself and others. Let it be a bright star that will lead you in your everyday life. Let it enrich your values, principles, morals, and beliefs.

- ❖ Existential well-being is finding something meaningful, finding inner peace, and discovering your purpose. Existential well-being is a personalized journey as well; it is not "one size fits all". Creating your own existential well-being could be as simple as taking a walk in the park or beach, enjoying nature, yoga, meditation, spending quiet time alone, being a part of community events, volunteering, appreciating life's small victories, creating, and enjoying hobbies.

There are so many things that you can do to create your existential well-being. I love helping people and offering acts of kindness. I give myself permission to glow through my smile, warm heart, and pleasantries, or what we call southern hospitality and positivity, and it shows in my everyday life. It comes back tenfold.

Treat Yourself

Treat yourself means just that. Do something good and pleasurable for yourself, but nothing that's necessary.

Be kind to yourself; you deserve it. Say it with me "I am deserving of kindness and treating myself!" Create your kindness as big or as small as you like. Here's a few of my favorite acts of kindness that help me restore my overall wellbeing.

- ❖ Facial pampering – big shout out to my friend and estheticians Portia McBride IG@skincarebyportia for always giving me the ultimate platinum level of facial experience, education in skincare, and extra gifts of skincare products contributing to my glowing face.

- Get-away – even if it's a day-cation, look in your area for places that offer day pass to enjoy resort amenities or make it a weekend getaway.

- Lunch, dinner, sweet treat – make it an experience, treat yourself to lunch or dinner, and enjoy the experience. Enjoy the flavors of the food, drinks, and dessert.

- Date night with yourself – appreciate yourself and pay gratitude to yourself for being your beautiful self. Light scented candles – my favorite Wild Orchid Candle Company, naturally derived eco-friendly blends of pure soy or coconut wax or LED lights, burn essential oils, have a glass of whatever is pleasing to your palate; mine is a glass of red wine. Take a long shower or relaxing rose petal bath. You can add a few drops of essential oils; use your imagination and create your own.

- Indulge in whatever makes you happy.

Seek Help

Here's a biggie of self-care: don't be afraid to seek help. Loving yourself requires you to take care of yourself by checking in with a medical provider annually. Seek professional help from a psychiatrist or psychologist. I encourage you to include visiting a board-certified dermatologist as well.

How Often Should You Visit a Board-Certificated Dermatologist?

You should always examine yourself for any changes in your skin. Skin Cancer Foundation (2023) recommends, "once a year, or more often if you are at a higher risk of skin cancer, for a full-body, professional skin exam."

Why is Dermatology Important?

Just to reiterate, the skin is the largest organ of the human body! So, why not? A Dermatologist is important because they are medical professionals who specialize in conditions that affect the skin. They are the skilled individuals that protect the largest organ of your body. They can detect whether it's a minor or major condition that can affect other underlying health conditions, like diabetes or heart disease which can show signs in your skin, hair, and nails. They hold unique skills in assisting with that healthy glowing face.

Remember early detection is the best line of defense in self-care. Don't take life for granted, because you only get one.

Give Yourself Permission to Glow

You should want to look and feel great, and you have the power to do so. Give yourself permission to glow. It's one of the essential components of a happy life. I shared with you all my granny's ingredients when it comes to starting fresh and even some of my favorite budget-friendly on-the-go products.

The key to having skin that glows lies deeper than the skin, so make those healthy deposits and invest wisely in your nutrition, hydration, and physical activity.

In today's world, there are a million and one things you are juggling. But reminder sleep is just like water; you need it to survive. Sleep allows the skin to heal, restore and rebuild, so invest in that quality beauty sleep.

I've given you a little science lesson when it comes to natural replenishment; the gift and curse of the sun. The main point is enjoy, be responsible, protect, again protect, and seek help if you notice any changes in the skin.

If you got nothing else from this book, I hope SELF-CARE left an impact of truly loving yourself mentally, physically and spiritually; taking time to appreciate yourself, giving yourself permission to glow, taking care of yourself and most importantly SEEKING HELP FROM A MEDICAL PROSESSIONAL.

Time has evolved in such a way that there are so many options to select from when it comes to facial care, but sometimes it's the basic things that are required. I've become a minimalist from traveling and working overseas, so for me, less is definitely better.

Think back to some of your family facial routines, have a good laugh, ask yourself why in the world they used them, research, and go back to basic natural concoctions.

TIME TO GLOW!

Works Cited

Wed document

Medically reviewed by Gerhard Whithwort R.N. - By Zawn Villines

- December 2018
- *Medical News Today website*
- 2023 Healthline Media UK LTD, Brighton, UK
- Accessed 16 June 2023
- Medicalnewstoday.com/articles/324039

By Mayo Clinic Staff

- 2022
- Mayo Clinic website

- *Mayo Foundation for Medical Education & Research (MFMER)*
- Accessed 16 June 2023
- Mayoclinic.org/healthy-lifestyle/nutrition-and-health-eating/indepth/water/art-20044256

Yazan Hamzah, Staff Writer

- January 2023
- *Sleep Foundation website*
- OneCare Media, LLC
- Accessed 16 June, 2023
- sleepfoundation.org/physical-health/beauty-sleep

Harrison Wein. PhD Editor; Tianna Hinklin, PhD Managing Editor; Alan Defibyh, Illustrator

- July 2014

- *NIH News In Health website*
- National Institutes of Health US Department of Health and Human Services
- Accessed 16 June 2023
- Newsinhealth.gov/2014/07/sun-skin

United States Environmental Protection Agency

- May 2023
- *EPA United States Environmental Protection Agency website*
- Accessed 16 June 2023
- United States Environmental Protection Agency
- epa.gov/sunsaftey/action-steps-sun-safety

Georgetown University Medical Center

- 2016
- *GU Georgetown University Medical Center website*
- Georgetown University Medical Center
- Accessed 16 June 2023
- gumc.georgetown.edu/news-release/sunlight-offers-surprise-benefit-it-energizes-infection-fighting-t-cells

Skin Cancer Foundation

- 2023
- *Skin Cancer website*
- The Skin Cancer Foundation A501(c)(3) Nonprofit Organization [EIN:13-2948778]
- Accessed 19 June 2023
- Skicancer.org/?s+self+exam

ACKNOWLEDGEMENT

To my support system, I am so grateful to my mom Evelyn and sister Tequila Hagan for their encouragement. This book is dedicated to my grandmother, but it is with great pleasure to share this book with both of you, as we laughed, laughed, and laughed going down memory lane.

To my mentors, where do I start? Mr. T.C. Chambers - Entrepreneur, Business Success Strategist (www.chartmydestiny.com)-IG@miamitc, this book would probably not be into existence without you. Thank you for speaking life into this project and for all your insight, wisdom, advice, time and support. Mr. Corey A. Harris - Entrepreneur, International Published Author, Breaking the Generational Curse (www.coreyaharris.net) Investor and, Athlete

IG@coreyaharris, a true testament to Ecclesiastes 3:1 "There is a time for everything, and season for every activity under the heavens." I first Thank God for placing you in my life at the right time and reason. Thank you for coaching and motivating me in the final phase of this book and other entrepreneurs' ventures. Your vast amount of support is immensely appreciated.

    To my friends and beautiful souls all over "Thank you" for supporting me. I hope this book was enlighten, informative and a pleasure to read. Peace, love and light

THE AUTHOR

Felecia Alexander is an enthusiast of living life to its fullest. She is commitment to living a healthy lifestyle through physical, mental, and spiritual well-being. She is most active in running, strength training, yoga, meditation, and self-care. Felecia is beautiful from the inside outward, her radiance shines everywhere so goes. She is a soul that speaks positive affirmation, a soul that loves helping others and offering acts of kindness, and most of all a soul believer that she can do all things through Christ. She hopes to enlighten and inspire you to **GLOW** in a healthy lifestyle.

Stay Connected

Website: www.u-glo.com

Instagram: @u.glo4u

www.ingramcontent.com/pod-product-compliance
Lightning Source LLC
LaVergne TN
LVHW061602070526
838199LV00077B/7151